1〇〇
GRACES

Also by Marcia and Jack Kelly

*SANCTUARIES: A Guide to Lodgings in
Monasteries, Abbeys, and Retreats
of the United States*
The Northeast
The West Coast and Southwest
The Complete United States

by Marcia Kelly

*HEAVENLY FEASTS: Memorable Meals from
Monasteries, Abbeys, and Retreats*

100 GRACES

MEALTIME BLESSINGS

SELECTED BY

Marcia and Jack Kelly

BELL TOWER / NEW YORK

For our friends and family, who are themselves a blessing

A percentage of the royalties from this book will go to the Seva Foundation (1786 5th Street, Berkeley, CA 94710) to help fund its worldwide program of compassionate action.

♦

Grateful acknowledgment is made for permission to reprint the graces on the following pages: 12, © 1992 by Robert Lax; 15, from *Kripalu Kitchen,* © Kripalu Yoga Fellowship 1980; 18, from *Complete Sayings of Hazrat Inayat Khan,* Omega Publications, Inc., New Lebanon, NY; 22, 35, and 46, © 1992 by Father John Giuliani; 24–6, from *To Be a Jew: A Guide to Jewish Observance in Contemporary Life* by Rabbi Hayim Halevy Donin, copyright © 1972 by the author. Reprinted by permission of Basic Books, a division of HarperCollins Publishers Inc.; 37–9 from *Present Moment, Wonderful Moment* by Thich Nhat Hanh, Parallax Press; 30, 70, and 77, from *Prayers for the Domestic Church* by Edward Hays, 1980, Forest of Peace Books Inc., Easton, Kansas; 48 and 74 from *The Tassajara Recipe Book* by Edward Espe Brown, Shambhala Publications; 52 and 61 copyright © 1991 by Evelyn Avoglia; 54, from *The Blessing Cup* by Rock Travnikar, OFM, St. Anthony Messenger Press; 67, from *Table Prayer* by M. D. Bouyer, The Crossroad Publishing Co., New York; 106, from *The Dhammapada,* copyright © 1976 by Thomas Byrom, Alfred A. Knopf, Inc; 110, from *Openings,* copyright © 1968 by Wendell Berry. Reprinted by permission of Harcourt Brace Jovanovich, Inc.

♦

Published by Bell Tower, an imprint of Harmony Books, a division of Crown Publishers, Inc., 201 East 50th Street, New York, New York 10022.
Member of the Crown Publishing Group.

Random House, Inc. New York, Toronto, London, Sydney, Auckland
http://www.randomhouse.com/

Bell Tower and colophon are trademarks of Crown Publishers, Inc.
Originally published by Bell Tower in hardcover in 1992 and in softcover in 1995

Printed in the United States of America

Design by June Bennett-Tantillo

Library of Congress Cataloging-in-Publication Data
One hundred graces/selected by Marcia and Jack Kelly;
p. cm.
1. Grace at meals. I. Kelly, Marcia. II. Kelly, Jack, 1934–
III 100 graces.
BV283.G7054 1992   242′.2—dc20   91-40464 CIP
ISBN 0-609-80093-0

10 9 8

✦ C O N T E N T S ✦

Saying grace is an ancient and vital tradition the world over. To begin with, it provides a space, a moment of stillness, in which to relinquish the activities of the day and allow the mind to settle. Then, as we acknowledge the source of our nourishment, we are filled with astonishment at the generosity of the Creator, with gratitude, and with praise. In bringing the body, mind, and heart together, we come to ourselves, and remember who we are and why we are here. For some families, a meal is the only time everyone is present and so the opportunity to enjoy one another and really celebrate the occasion is not to be lost. For many, a meal is also the only time that there is any memory of the Divine. Saying grace establishes an immediate connection with that memory. In such a moment, when our minds are clear and the truth is reinforced by being sounded aloud, we can dedicate the meal and the strength we receive from it to the service of whoever or whatever is before us.

GRACE

BY ROBERT LAX

Grace
be
fore
breath
ing

grace
while
breath
ing

grace
af
ter
breath
ing

be
fore
eat
ing

af
ter
eat
ing

while
eat
ing

grace
be
fore
each
good
&
need
ed
ac
tion

each
ac
tiv
i
ty

grace
at
eve
ry

mo
ment

of
our
lives

grace
be
fore
dy
ing

grace
be
fore
birth

thanks
&
bless
ing

to
ac
com
pan
y

eve
ry
mo
ment

of
our
lives

grace
ful
grace

grace
grace-
giving

calls
forth
bless
ing

&
gives
thanks

for
bless
ings

grace
is
thanks

our
thanks

for
every

bless
ing

grace
be
fore

dream
ing

grace
be
fore
sleep

grace
while
dream
ing

grace
in
sleep

grace
af
ter
dream
ing

grace
af
ter
sleep

grace
for
the
bless
ing

of
dreams
&
sleep

grace
is
bless
ing

a
thanks
for
bless
ing

a
thanks
for
be
ing
a
ble

to
thank

for
bless
ings

for
be
ing

so
blessed

for
be
ing

so
graced

as
to
be

ev
er

a
ble

to
thank

for
grace

❖

❖

AFFIRMATION TO MY BODY

I recognize you are the temple in which
my spirit and creative energy dwell.

❖

I have created you from my need to have
my spirit manifest on earth so that I may
have this time to learn and grow.

❖

I offer you this food so that you may continue to
sustain my creative energy, my spirit, my soul.

❖

I offer this food to you with love, and
a sincere desire for you to remain free from
disease and disharmony.

❖

I accept you as my own creation.

❖

I need you.

❖

I love you.

FROM KRIPALU KITCHEN

BE present at our table, Lord.
Be here and everywhere adored.
Thy creatures bless and grant that we
May feast in Paradise with Thee.

➤ JOHN CENNICK (1718–1755)

On the Upper West Side of New York City there is a wonderful group called Project Reachout (a project of Goddard-Riverside Community Center), who work with the homeless people who are mentally ill. At their special program, "The Other Place," a theatrical session was held and the topic was mealtime graces. Nineteen of the members present that day* had a grace to contribute. This was one of them.

*GEORGE, GARY, DUSTY, ANTON, LEO, JOE, BARBARA, BILLY, PHIL, FLORENCE, FRANK, BRADLEY, LAVERNE, CARL, MARIA, MARSHALL, MANUEL, GREGORY, PHILIP, JOHN, DIANE, ED, NELIDA.

⇥BE⇤

the eye of God betwixt me and each eye,
the purpose of God betwixt me and each purpose,
the hand of God betwixt me and each hand,
the shield of God betwixt me and each shield,
the desire of God betwixt me and each desire,
the bridle of God betwixt me and each bridle,
And no mouth can curse me.
The pain of Christ betwixt me and each pain,
the love of Christ betwixt me and each love,
the dearness of Christ betwixt me and each dearness,
the kindness of Christ betwixt me and each kindness,
the wish of Christ betwixt me and each wish,
the will of Christ betwixt me and each will,
And no venom can wound me.

◆

For centuries it was the custom in Scotland to say a blessing before any action. This is one of the Gaelic graces collected by Alexander Carmichael in the nineteenth century and used in Avery Brooke's *Celtic Prayers*.

BELOVED

Lord, almighty God,
through the rays of the sun
through the waves of the air
through the all-pervading life in space
purify and revivify me,
and, I pray, heal my body, heart, and soul.
Amen.

◆ *NAYAZ* BY HAZRAT INAYAT KHAN

BELOVED

Lord, we do greatly thank You
for the abundance
that is ours.

BISMILLAH

al-Rahman al-Rahim

❖

(In the name of
the compassionate
and beneficent God)

❖

TRANSLATION BY DR. ADIL H. AL-HUMADI

❖

This Islamic invocation is used before any action, but particularly before meals. It is said that Muhammad (peace be upon him) recited a longer form of this blessing: "O Lord, bless this food and protect us from the doom of fire. In the name of God we begin our meal."

BLESS,

O Lord,
this food
to our use
and us
to Thy
loving
service.

———•◦•———

BLESS our hearts to hear in the breaking of bread the song of the universe.

◆ FATHER JOHN GIULIANI
  THE BENEDICTINE GRANGE
  WEST REDDING, CONNECTICUT

BLESSED

are You,
O Lord our God,
Eternal King,
Who feeds the whole world
With Your goodness,
With grace, with loving kindness,
And with tender mercy.

You give food to all flesh,
For Your loving kindness endures forever.
Through Your great goodness,
Food has never failed us.
O may it not fail us forever,
For Your name's sake, since You
Nourish and sustain all living things
And do good to all,
And provide food for all Your creatures
Whom You have created.

Blessed are You, O Lord,
Who gives food to all.

➤ A HEBREW *BERAKHAH* (BLESSING)

BLESSED

art Thou, O Lord our God,
King of the universe, through
whose word all things were
called into being.

♦

FROM *TO BE A JEW:
A GUIDE TO JEWISH OBSERVANCE
IN CONTEMPORARY LIFE*
BY RABBI HAYIM HALEVY DONIN

BLESSED

art Thou, O Lord our God,
King of the universe,
who creates many living
beings and the things they
need. For all that Thou hast
created to sustain
the life of every living
being, blessed be Thou,
the Life of the universe.

FROM *TO BE A JEW*
BY RABBI HAYIM HALEVY DONIN

BLESSED art Thou, O Lord our God, King of the universe, who has kept us in life and sustained us and enabled us to reach this season.

➤ FROM *TO BE A JEW*
BY RABBI HALIM HALEVY DONIN

COME, let us
welcome the Sabbath.
May its radiance illumine our
hearts as we kindle these tapers.

❖

May the Lord bless us with Sabbath
joy.

❖

May the Lord bless us with Sabbath
holiness.

❖

May the Lord bless us with Sabbath
peace.

❖

This grace is said in a traditional Jewish home before the meal on
Friday evening, as the candles are lit to welcome the Sabbath.

COME, Lord Jesus!

I open my mind and heart and soul,
And long for You to be born anew in me.
Help me to experience Your presence within me,
And to allow You to touch the earth through me.

Come, Lord Jesus!
Come and stay with my family and friends
And all who are dear to me. Be near
Especially those who are burdened by
Sickness or sadness. Set them free
By Your love and care.

Come, Lord Jesus!
Bring peace to our world. May we hear again
Your own prayer: "That we may be one."
And may we learn anew to follow Your example:
"That there may be bread" for all.

We hunger, we thirst, we wait for You!
Come, Lord Jesus!
And do not delay!

THIS ADVENT prayer comes from SALLIE LATKOVICH, CSJ, OF THE MOTHER OF GOD HOUSE OF PRAYER IN ALVA, FLORIDA

CREATOR,

Earth Mother,
we thank You for our lives and
this beautiful day. Thank You for the bright sun
and the rain we received last night.
Thank You for this circle of friends
and the opportunity to be together.
We want to thank You especially at this time
for the giveaway of their lives made by the
chickens, beets, carrots, grains, and lettuce.
We thank them for giving of their lives
so we may continue our lives through this
great blessing. Please help us honor them
through how we live our lives.

◆

MARY FALLAHAY OF THE BEAR TRIBE MEDICINE SOCIETY,
SPOKANE, WASHINGTON

This grace was created in honor of the meal we had together
on May 2, 1991.

THE day is coming to a close,
and, like the disciples on the road to Emmaus,
we pause to break bread together.
May our eyes be opened,
and, in this act of common sharing,
may we see the Risen Lord in one another.
May we see the Lord of Life in our food,
our conversation, and lives shared in common.
May the blessing of God,
His peace and love,
rest upon our table.
Alleluia! Amen.

→ EVENING MEAL BLESSING FOR EASTER
BY EDWARD HAYS OF SHANTIVANAM, EASTON, KANSAS

DEAREST Lord,

teach me to be generous.
Teach me to serve Thee as Thou
   deservest;
To give and not to count the cost;
To fight and not to heed the wounds;
To toil and not to seek reward,
Save that of knowing that
I do Thy will, O God.

ST. IGNATIUS LOYOLA (1491–1556)

❖

DEEP peace of the shining
star to you,
Deep peace of the running wave to you,
Deep peace of the quiet earth to you,
Deep joy of the leaping fire to you,
Deep peace of the Son of Peace to you.

◆ CELTIC PRAYER FROM SISTER SUSAN,
NADA HERMITAGE, CRESTONE, COLORADO

❖

EAT your bread
with joy and drink with
a merry heart, because
it is now that God favors
your works.

➤ MOUNT ST. MARY'S ABBEY,
WRENTHAM, MASSACHUSETTS

THE eyes of all wait upon Thee

and Thou gives them their meat in due season.
Thou openest Thy hand
and fillest all things living with plenteousness.

We thank Thee, O Lord, for these Thy gifts
and beseech Thee to grant that whether we eat
or drink or whatsoever we do, all may be done
to Thy glory.

At some monasteries the first four lines—which are from Psalm 104,
verses 27 and 28—are read responsively.

· 34 ·

FAITHFUL God,

let this table be a sign of tomorrow's
hope already here, when with the world
which hungers for Your justice and peace,
we shall come together, singing Your
name as our very own.

FATHER JOHN GIULIANI,
THE BENEDICTINE GRANGE,
WEST REDDING, CONNECTICUT

❖ FATHER, ❖

bless this food which
re-creates our bodies.
May the hearing of Your
word re-create our souls.

❖

MOUNT ST. MARY'S ABBEY,
WRENTHAM, MASSACHUSETTS

FIVE *GATHAS*

BY THE VIETNAMESE BUDDHIST MONK,
THICH NHAT HANH

———◦◦◦———

SERVING FOOD

◆

I n this food I see clearly
the presence of the entire universe
supporting my existence.

LOOKING AT THE PLATE
FILLED WITH FOOD

◆

ALL living beings are struggling for life. May they all have enough food to eat today.

JUST BEFORE EATING

◆

THE plate is filled with food. I am aware that each morsel is the fruit of much hard work by those who produced it.

BEGINNING TO EAT

◆

WITH the first taste, I promise to practice loving kindness.
With the second, I promise to relieve the suffering of others.
With the third, I promise to see others' joy as my own.
With the fourth, I promise to learn the way of nonattachment and equanimity.

This verse is said while taking the first four mouthfuls of food. They are a reminder of the Four Immeasurable States: loving kindness, compassion, sympathetic joy, and nonattachment.

FINISHING THE MEAL

◆

THE plate is empty. My hunger is satisfied. I vow to live for the benefit of all beings.

FOOD–

God's love made edible.
May we be swept into
Your presence.

❦

BROTHER THOMAS, NADA HERMITAGE,
CRESTONE, COLORADO

FOR each new morning with
   its light,
For rest and shelter of the night,
For health and food, for love and friends,
For everything Thy goodness sends.

➤ RALPH WALDO EMERSON (1803–1882)

GIVE food to the hungry, O Lord, and hunger for You to those who have food.

GIVE us this day

our daily bread, O Father
in heaven, and grant that we
who are filled with good things
from Your open hand
may never close our hearts
to the hungry, the homeless,
and the poor;
in the name of the Father,
and of the Son,
and of the Holy Spirit.

•—◆—•

ABBEY OF NEW CLAIRVAUX,
VINA, CALIFORNIA

GIVE us this day
our daily bread, O Father
in heaven, and grant that we
who gather here in fellowship of faith and love may
take our food with gladness
and simplicity of heart.

➤ ABBEY OF NEW CLAIRVAUX,
VINA, CALIFORNIA

GOD, I thank You for the blessings and gifts that You have provided for me and my relatives, and the food that You have provided also. I pray that we will receive strength and good health from it. So be it.

◆ LAKOTA GRACE
TRANSLATED BY BILL QUEJAS

GOD of pilgrims,
give us always a table to
stop at where we can
tell our story and
sing our song.

❖

FATHER JOHN GIULIANI,
THE BENEDICTINE GRANGE,
WEST REDDING, CONNECTICUT

❖

GOD to enfold me, God to surround me,

God in my speaking, God in my thinking.
God in my sleeping, God in my waking,
God in my watching, God in my hoping.
God in my life, God in my lips,
God in my soul, God in my heart.
God in my sufficing, God in my slumber,
God in mine ever-living soul, God in mine
   serenity.

THIS GAELIC GRACE WAS COLLECTED
BY ALEXANDER CARMICHAEL IN THE
NINETEENTH CENTURY AND USED
IN AVERY BROOKE'S *CELTIC PRAYERS*

I do this chore not just to get it out of the way but as the way to make real kind connected mind.

May I awaken to what these ingredients offer, and may I awaken as best I can energy, warmth, imagination, this offering of heart and hand.

FROM *THE TASSAJARA RECIPE BOOK* BY EDWARD ESPE BROWN

I offer You this day
All I shall think, do, say for:
(peace in the world)

❖

(Everyone at the table then states
his or her own intention for the day.)

❖

DON GEORGE, LA CASA DE MARIA,
SANTA BARBARA, CALIFORNIA

I slept and dreamt
that life was joy,
I awoke and saw
that life was service.
I acted and behold,
service was joy.

RABINDRANATH TAGORE (1861–1941)

I was regretting the past
and fearing the future.
Suddenly God was speaking.
"My name is 'I am.'" I waited.
God continued,
"When you live in the past,
with its mistakes and regrets,
it is hard. I am not there.
My name is not 'I was.'
When you live in the future,
with its problems and fears, it is hard.
I am not there.
My name is not 'I will be.'
When you live in this moment,
it is not hard. I am here.
My name is 'I am.'"

➤ FROM HELEN MELLICOST
(ON THE KITCHEN WALL OF THE
RANCH GUESTHOUSE, ST. BENEDICT'S
MONASTERY, SNOWMASS, COLORADO)

I will sing to You, O sing to You.
You have been good to me.

Air and fire, earth and water
Reveal Your face to me.
O Maker of the universes,
You have been good to me.

War and famine, peace and plenty
Reveal Your face to me.
God of time and endless ages,
You have been good to me.

Song and story, word and wonder
Reveal Your face to me.
Holy Wisdom of all nations,
You have been good to me.

Hands and labor, hearts and longing
Reveal Your face to me.
Loving Maker of the people,
You have been good to me.

EVELYN AVOGLIA OF BRIDGEPORT, CONNECTICUT,
WROTE THIS "SONG OF THE FOUR SCRIPTURES"
BASED ON A LECTURE BY FATHER THOMAS BERRY

IN India, when we meet and part
we often say "*Namaste*,"*
which means I honor the place in you
where the entire universe resides.
I honor the place in you
of love, of light, of truth, of peace.
I honor the place within you where,
if you are in that place in you
and I am in that place in me,
there is only one of us.

➤ FROM *GRIST FOR THE MILL* BY RAM DASS

* PRONOUNCED *NAMASTAY*.

IN the spirit of humble prayer
we give thanks.

For our family, friends, relatives,
and those who teach us of God's way,
◆ we pray. ◆
We thank You, Lord, for our home and for the
many things You surround us with in goodness,
◆ we pray. ◆
For all creation, for sights and sounds
and all our senses,
◆ we pray. ◆

(Anyone at the table may add
a petition or request after this.)

◆

FROM *THE BLESSING CUP*
BY ROCK TRAVNIKAR, OFM

EVERYONE

at the table joins hands

for a silent moment.

❖

QUAKER GRACE

JUST to be is a blessing.
Just to live is holy.

ABRAHAM JOSHUA HESCHEL

KNOW, too, from Me

Shineth the gathered glory of the suns
Which lighten all the world: from Me the
    moons
Draw silvery beams, and fire fierce loveliness.
I penetrate the clay, and lend all shapes
Their living force; I glide into the plant—
Root, leaf, and bloom—to make the woodlands
    green
With springing sap. Becoming vital warmth,
I glow in glad, respiring frames, and pass,
With outward and with inward breath,
    to feed
The body by all meats.

➤ THE SONG CELESTIAL OR BHAGAVAD GITA
TRANSLATED FROM THE SANSKRIT
BY SIR EDWIN ARNOLD

LET

there be peace on earth
and let it begin with me.
Let there be peace on earth
and let it begin with me.
Let there be peace on earth
and let it begin with me.

Peace in our food,
Peace in our bodies,
Peace in our home,
Peace in our world,
Thanks, God.
Amen.

◆ The Rev. Dr. Barbara King,
   Hillside International Truth Center,
   Atlanta, Georgia

LET this food bless us, heal us, balance us, energize us, and put us in harmony with everything good in the universe.

❖

THEO LEVINE AND SONYA HELLER

LET us give thanks for this food
And Thy blessing and benediction be upon it.
May our hands so energize this food
That it supplies the needs of our bodies
And may we be moved to share with others
What they are in need of.

⁓ THIS BLESSING, FROM THE SAKYA MONASTERY
IN SEATTLE, WASHINGTON, IS SAID WITH EVERYONE
RAISING THEIR HANDS (PALMS DOWN) OVER THE FOOD.

LISTEN, my soul.

This is your task:
To bless the holy name of Yahweh and
remember all God's kindnesses.
Remember your offenses and know
they are forgiven.
Remember your diseases and know
that they are healed.
Remember your death and know
that you are living.
Know that this tender love is
Yahweh's way with you.
A fool may ask for justice, but
Yahweh gives us mercy.
Our sins deserve God's anger, but
we are given love.
All within me sings:
Yahweh is our loving God
Whose mercy is upon us; bless your God,
my soul.

•◆•

EVELYN AVOGLIA OF BRIDGEPORT, CONNECTICUT,
WAS INSPIRED TO WRITE THIS THROUGH READING THE PSALMS.

LORD, bless our meal, and as You satisfy the needs of each of us, make us mindful of the needs of others.

◆ MOUNT ST. MARY'S ABBEY,
  WRENTHAM, MASSACHUSETTS

LORD, bless our shared meal, a sacrament to our shared unity.

MOUNT ST. MARY'S ABBEY,
WRENTHAM, MASSACHUSETTS

THE Lord bless you

❖ and keep you: ❖

The Lord make His face to shine upon
you, and be gracious unto you:
The Lord lift up His countenance upon
you, and give you peace.

❖

NUMBERS 6: 24–26

This was the blessing bestowed upon the people in the ancient temple
by the high priest, as commanded in the *Torah*. Today it is incorporated
into the service by the rabbi or by descendants of the ancient holy families. If the person giving this blessing is very observant and pious, it is
accompanied by a special hymn and sung with the face covered by a *tal-
lit* (prayer shawl). A favorite childhood Sunday school teacher, Joseph
M. Bear, explained this to us recently. Little did he expect to be our
teacher well into adulthood.

LORD,

make me an instrument of Your peace.
Where there is hatred, let me sow love;
where there is injury, pardon;
where there is doubt, faith;
where there is darkness, light;
and where there is sadness, joy.
O Divine Master, grant that I may
not so much seek to be consoled as to console;
to be understood as to understand;
to be loved as to love,
for it is in giving that we receive,
it is in pardoning that we are pardoned,
and it is in dying that we are born to eternal life.

ST. FRANCIS OF ASSISI
(1182?–1226)

LORD our God,

You invite us to the banquet of Your wisdom, giving us for nourishment both the bread of the earth and Your living word. Bless this meal, and grant us entry to Your banquet. In the name of the Father, and of the Son, and of the Holy Spirit. Amen.

• ◆ •

FROM *TABLE PRAYER* BY M. D. BOUYER

LORD,

we begin this meal by giving thanks to You.
This food is the gift of Your creation.
Protect that creation from all harm and hatred.
May we cherish the earth and all who partake
of its richness.
May we choose life and peace
so that we and all Your children may live.
We offer our thanks to You, our God of peace,
through Jesus, the Prince of Peace.
Amen.

SCJ OFFICE OF JUSTICE AND PEACE,
PRIESTS OF THE SACRED HEART,
HALES CORNERS, WISCONSIN

LORD, we have been
nourished by our meal
and by Your presence with us.
Give us the strength to build
a unity of love
among ourselves and friends
and others.
Help us to grow in Your ways,
which are the ways of peace.
We offer this prayer through Jesus,
who is our Way, our Truth,
and our Life.
Amen.

❖

SCJ OFFICE OF JUSTICE AND PEACE,
PRIESTS OF THE SACRED HEART,
HALES CORNERS, WISCONSIN

LORD, You who gave
bread to Moses and his people
while they traveled in the desert,
come now, and bless these gifts of food
which You have given to us.
As this food gives up its life for us,
may we follow that pattern of
self-surrender for each other.
May we be life to one another.

➤ FROM *PRAYERS FOR THE DOMESTIC CHURCH*
BY EDWARD HAYS

MAY all beings have happiness
and the causes of happiness.
May all beings be free from sorrow
and the causes of sorrow.
May all never be separated from the sacred
happiness which is sorrowless.
May all live in equanimity, without
attachment or aversion,
believing in the equality of all that lives.

◆

NYINGMA INSTITUTE,
BERKELEY, CALIFORNIA

MAY

God bless our meal
and grant us a compassionate
and understanding heart
toward one another.

➤ MOUNT ST. MARY'S ABBEY,
WRENTHAM, MASSACHUSETTS

MAY He who comes
bless our meal
and enable us to discern
His coming
in every grace-filled moment
of our lives.

MOUNT ST. MARY'S ABBEY,
WRENTHAM, MASSACHUSETTS

MAY I

together with
all beings,
enjoy the pure taste
of kind mind
joyful mind
big mind.

♦ FROM *THE TASSAJARA RECIPE BOOK*
   BY EDWARD ESPE BROWN

MAY light and love surround us and guide us to right action.

❖

A BLESSING GIVEN TO OUR FRIEND,
LINDA MOSCARELLA,
AT A MEETING AT THE UNIVERSALIST CHURCH,
NEW YORK CITY

MAY love, joy, and peace be yours in abundance.

LARRY AND GIRIJA BRILLIANT

MAY our home be made holy,
O God, by Your light.
May the light of love and truth shine
upon us all as a blessing from You.
May our table and our family
be consecrated by Your Divine Presence
at this meal and
at all our family meals.
Amen.

• ◆ •

FROM *PRAYERS FOR THE DOMESTIC CHURCH*
BY EDWARD HAYS

This blessing is recited as the candles are lit for the Jewish sabbath.

MAY prayerful peace
flow outward from here,
touching with grace
all those whom you love
and all the earth as well.
Amen.

◆

Our Lady of Solitude House of Prayer,
Black Canyon City, Arizona

MAY the blessing of God
rest upon you,
May His peace abide with you,
May His presence illuminate your heart
Now and forevermore.

🐝 SUFI BLESSING

O M

MAY the Gods through our
senses enjoy this food.

May we always be just a witness
and let the food nourish and strengthen
our bodies and minds so that we can
climb up to the last step of Yoga.
(Bliss, self-realization,
God-realization, *samadhi*)
Om shanti, shanti, shanti

◆

THIS MEALTIME BLESSING IS USED BY DHARMA MITRA
AT SPECIAL CELEBRATIONS WITH HIS YOGA STUDENTS IN NEW YORK

Om is a sacred syllable which both embraces all things and is the cause of their creation. It is often sounded at the commencement and conclusion of a prayer: The lips are rounded and the sound "O" rises steadily from deep in the body. The lips gradually close in a strong humming which resonates in the nose. The Sanskrit word *shanti* is pronounced with a long "a," as in "ah," and a very short lilting "i." Repeated thrice in this way, it can be understood to mean "May peace and peace and peace be everywhere." Generally all present join in sounding *Om* even if the rest of the grace is spoken by one person.

MAY the Lord accept this, our offering, and bless our food that it may bring us strength in our body, vigor in our mind, and selfless devotion in our heart for His service.

➤ SWAMI PARAMANANDA,
BOOK OF DAILY THOUGHTS AND PRAYER

›MAY‹

the words

of our mouths

and the meditations

of our hearts

be acceptable

in Thy sight,

O Lord.

◆

PSALM 19:14

MAY there always be work for your hands to do.

❖

May your purse always hold a coin or two.

❖

May the sun always shine upon your window pane.

❖

May a rainbow be certain to follow each rain.

❖

May the hand of a friend always be near to you and

❖

May God fill your heart with gladness to cheer you.

AN IRISH BLESSING

MAY we be
a channel of blessings
for all that we meet.

꩜

EDGAR CAYCE

NOW that I am about to eat,

O Great Spirit, give my thanks to the beasts and birds whom You have provided for my hunger, and pray deliver my sorrow that living things must make a sacrifice for my comfort and well-being. Let the feather of corn spring up in its time and let it not wither but make full grains for the fires of our cooking pots, now that I am about to eat.

♦ A Native American grace
from the Lama Foundation,
San Cristobal, New Mexico

O God, bless this food
we are about to receive.
Give bread to those who
hunger; and hunger
for justice to us
who have bread.
Amen.

∽⚬∾

This grace is used in many places around the world. One source said that it
came from Nicaragua and another that it was part of the liturgy of the
French Community of the Ark, a working order of men and women who
put into daily practice Gandhi's principles of nonviolence and dedication
to truth.

O God, You are the giver of every good and perfect gift. We are aware of how easily we take and how often we grudgingly give. Give us the gift of grateful hearts, that we may want to share freely with others all You have given us.
Amen.

➤ St. Paul the Apostle Monastery,
Palm Desert, California

Ogracious God, when You open
Your hand,
You satisfy the desires of every living thing.
Bless the land and waters;
give the world a plentiful harvest;
let Your spirit go forth to renew the face of
the earth.
As You show Your love and kindness
in the bounty of the land and sea,
save us from selfish use of Your gifts,
so that women and men everywhere
may give You thanks,
for Jesus' sake.
Amen.

❖

HOLDEN VILLAGE,
CHELAN, WASHINGTON

O Lord God, who
has called us Your servants
to ventures of which
we cannot see the ending,
by paths as yet untrodden
and through perils unknown:
Give us faith to go out with
good courage, not knowing
where we go, but only that
Your hand is leading us
and Your love supporting us.
Amen.

HOLDEN VILLAGE,
CHELAN, WASHINGTON

O Thou who clothes the lilies,
Who feeds the birds of the sky,
Who leads the lambs to pasture,
And the deer to the waterside,
Who multiplied loaves and fishes,
And changed the water to wine,
Do Thou come to our table as giver
And as our guest to dine.

ONCE they saw a star

that pointed to a promised land, to a land of peace, peacemakers set out to follow that star.

It is both a joyful and arduous journey. Sometimes the star shines brightly, the promise seems certain, and the pilgrims can sing, "How beautiful are the feet of those who bring God's peace." Often the star disappears, clouded over, hidden from view, and the pilgrims grope blindly, grow discouraged, get weary, give thought to settling down, to forgetting the promise of peace.

One thing is certain: All pilgrims need nourishment to sustain the journey. An occasional oasis for the spirit is essential, a time to feast on the refreshing waters, the rich food of the spirit, in order to get strength to continue the pilgrimage through darkness, star-shine or not.

♦ MARY LOU KOWNACKI, OSB,
OF THE CATHOLIC PEACE MOVEMENT,
PAX CHRISTI USA, ERIE, PENNSYLVANIA

OUR Father, we are
grateful for this family,
who hand in hand form
one unbroken circle.
Help us to do Thy will,
as caring individuals and
as a loving family.
Amen.

———◆———

PRAISE,

praise to the Father,
Praise, praise to the Son,
Praise, praise to the Spirit,
All praise to the Three in One.

❖

Bless each of our families.
Bless this food we eat.
May we be a blessing
To all that we meet.
Amen.

❖

CHRISTIAN RENEWAL CENTER,
SILVERTON, OREGON

PRAISE to the Lord of all creation,
Glory to God, the fount of grace;
May peace abide in every nation,
Goodwill to all of every race.

ALL

who are at the table
raise their plates
for a quiet moment.

❖

RECALL the face
of the poorest and most helpless man whom
you may have seen and ask yourself if the step
you contemplate is going to be of any use to
him. Will it restore him to a control over his own
life and destiny? Will it lead to self-rule for the
hungry and spiritually starved millions of our
fellow men? If so, then you will find your doubts
and yourself melting away.

THE GANDHI TALISMAN

THE

 seed of God is in us. Given an intelligent and hardworking farmer, it will thrive and grow up into God, whose seed it is; and accordingly its fruits will be God-nature. Pear seeds grow into pear trees, nut seeds into nut trees, and God seeds into God.

◆ MEISTER ECKHART
(1260–1329)

❖

SING to God,
sing praises to His name.
Lift up a song to Him
who rides upon the clouds;
His name is the Lord.
Exalt before Him.

❖

PSALM 68:4

THE SELKIRK GRACE

SOME hae meat,
and canna eat,
And some wad eat that want it,
But we hae meat and we can eat,
And sae the Lord be thankit.

◆ ROBERT BURNS

THANK

Heaven for this food
and for this company.
May it be good for us.

DAMIANOS THEODOSIOS,
PATMOS, GREECE

THANKS

to Thee, O God, that I have risen today.
To the rising of this life itself;
May it be to Thine own glory,
O God of every gift,
And to the glory of my soul likewise.
O great God, aid Thou my soul
With the aiding of Thine own mercy;
Even as I clothe my body with wool,
Cover Thou my soul with the shadow of
  Thy wing.
Help me to avoid every sin,
And the source of every sin to forsake;
And as the mist scatters on the crest of
  the hills,
May each ill haze clear from my soul,
  O God.

➤ THIS GAELIC GRACE WAS COLLECTED
BY ALEXANDER CARMICHAEL
IN THE NINETEENTH CENTURY AND USED
IN AVERY BROOKE'S *CELTIC PRAYERS*.

→THERE←

is only one caste,

the caste of humanity;

There is only one religion,

the religion of love;

There is only one language,

the language of the heart.

◆

SATHYA SAI BABA

THIS is a time for giving thanks.

This is a time for remembrance.

❖

Let us remember all those
who are united with us and
give thanks for that bond of union . . .

❖

Let us remember our past and
give thanks for what we have become . . .

❖

Let us be present in the present and
give thanks for the here-and-now . . .

❖

Let us remember our future and
give thanks for all that is to happen to us . . .

❖

Let us give thanks for the whole universe,
especially for our creation and the life that
    is in us . . .

❖

Let us give thanks for that consummation
    of all things
which the Spirit is working out in us.

❖

Thank You!

THIS

is a time of chaos.
This is a time for healing.
This is a time of choice.
This is a time to care.
This is a time to stand and say "yes."
This is a time to stand and say "no."
This is a time of challenge.
This is a time for peace.

THE
CALL
TO
COMMON
GROUND

We join together,
old and young,
frail and strong,
hearts and hands,
to heal the wounds
we have wrought for centuries.

There is blood in our waters,
acid in our land,
death in our skies.

We join together to take up
the sword of truth
and the shield of light
to dissolve all boundaries,
deceit, and judgment,
to stand united once again—I and thou
in the garden of brotherhood.
The human heart is common ground.

FROM *COMMON
GROUND,* 1991,
BY SARAH RIELY,
PUBLISHER,
*CONNECTING
ARIZONA,* PHOENIX,
ARIZONA

THIS ritual is One.
The food is One.
We who offer the food are One.
The fire of hunger is also One.
All action is One.
We who understand this are One.

❖

AN ANCIENT HINDU BLESSING BEFORE MEALS

❖

WE are what we think.
All that we are arises with our thoughts.
With our thoughts we make the world.
Speak or act with an impure mind
and trouble will follow you
as the wheel follows the ox that draws the cart.
Speak or act with a pure mind
and happiness will follow you
As your shadow, unshakable.

•◆•

FROM *THE DHAMMAPADA: THE SAYINGS OF THE BUDDHA,*
RENDERED INTO ENGLISH BY THOMAS BYROM

WE cannot love God unless we love each other, and to love each other we must know each other in the breaking of bread and we are not alone anymore. Heaven is a banquet and life is a banquet, too, even with a crust, where there is companionship. Love comes with community.

⚜ DOROTHY DAY

WE come to join
in the banquet of love.
Let it open our hearts
and break down the fears
that keep us from loving each other.

◆

SUNG BY DOMINICAN NUNS
ON SPECIAL OCCASIONS AT MEALTIME

WE thank Thee
for our daily bread.
Let, also, Lord,
our souls be fed.
O, Bread of Life,
from day to day
sustain us on our
homeward way.
Amen.

❧

THE ECKHARDT FAMILY

THE PEACE OF WILD THINGS

WHEN despair for the
world grows in me
and I wake in the night at the least sound
in fear of what my life and my children's
lives may be,
I go and lie down where the wood drake
rests in his beauty on the water, and the
great heron feeds.
I come into the peace of wild things
who do not tax their lives with forethought
of grief.
I come into the presence of still water.
And I feel above me the day-blind stars
waiting with their light.
For a time I rest in the grace of the world,
and am free.

◆ WENDELL BERRY

⋄ WHERE ⋄

two or three are gathered together
in Thy name, Thou has promised
to be in their midst. Grant that we
may be channels for Thy love in
the world and awaken our souls to the
knowledge of Thy healing powers.

And may the peace of joy be with you.

⋄

INDRALAYA, EASTSOUND, WASHINGTON

This prayer is used to send healing thoughts. Visualize the person
who needs to be healed and speak the name of that person aloud before
saying the final line of the prayer.

Marcia and Jack Kelly are writers who live in New York City. Their books include the series *Sanctuaries: A Guide to Lodgings in Monasteries, Abbeys, and Retreats of the United States* and *Heavenly Feasts: Memorable Meals from Monasteries, Abbeys, and Retreats.* Their research has so far taken them to more than two hundred and fifty monasteries, and many of the graces in this book were collected on these travels.